A Preventive Measure to
help Stop Manmade Disasters
(A way to save multitudes of people from harm)

An analogy: are we a people who just do not want to understand the freedom we need at this time because we have had too much already?

Dedication

Dedicated to my Dad:

If you are on a dinghy that is sailing through the air with clear waters to sew and mend the brokenness in people on the earthly place to not come apart.

A Rebirth of Discipleship in America

We are looking for those on or off the highways and byways who think they can't be used by the Lord in his melting pot, the land of the free the home of the brave.

This is a way to repair the damage and clean things up so the star spangled banner can shine new because our image has been hit to the curve.

This is for the people who don't like change and would rather stay in the wilderness. I love you too in the name of my Savior Jesus Christ and you can do something about it. Try this and see how you feel.

Do we see this as ironic? Why other nations feel like they do about us. Or can we accept it as a part of our sanity? Or is it a form of insanity that will turn out right? If the premises of fake news has related to our latest presidential election and was developed by the Russians, who had the indication that we (meaning Hillary Clinton) developed it to create controversy during the Putin regime that he felt she causing mass confusion in there county, that gave use a dose of our medicine is it because of guilt in our nation that it has been reversed on us because we started this country using fake news to take and steal land from native people?

It is also time to wake up and understand if you are not rich in the USA that the government is still putting fake news out to us. They treat the uneducated and less fortunate like they are peons. They have been doing it ever since it was being taken from the nation's people and it hasn't stopped. Even when you look at the new tax bill that passed. The more they get the less you get. The towerists say it is for the people. But again fake news even hit the black people with 40 acres and a mule.

Facing another conundrum to build the knowledge we have to set forth a peace that requires the right material to be developed and it is not just in one book but several that may be twins, triplets or even as many as seven to make up one presentation of knowledge.

Now one of the people's biggest problems in people's lives is they don't want to be made to look wrong to others as pride is taking on a new face that leads to a dark side inside of them.

To the Public at Large

Can this knowledge be noted as one of the best ways

to help insure that America comes back in a new kind of spiritual light with grace?

If you are tired of hearing about someone else's life in a book or whatever, it may be time to learn how to re-right your life and future to self and others with one of Bound to Heaven Publishing/Ministries' books.

Be it Known

One of the nastiest words ever said is crazyism. It is not supposed to be real but it is now like a plague in our land that we can stop from happening more. There are some tidbits of information that came out of other books that I have authored.

This is a forerunner to discipleship to help make American people great first. Know now we can bypass the mandatory sentence that Satan uses from being misused and abused that takes our time to unchain us from the taxing lifestyle that causes us problems.

Today, I would like to bring wisdom to a full circle and let the world know what the one man wrecking ball, Donald Trump, has and that is towerism that makes him act like a man baby within some of his actions so other people in other lands can somewhat understand what over one half of the people of the USA are putting up with and maybe it can help keep the peace, at least until he gets out of office after his term. That is why The *Calm During the Storm*, *Fixing What is Broken in America by Stopping Towerism*, plus at the start I use the premises in the book peace at the RNC, *The Devil Passed Me By*, *Ending Political Wars in America*, *A Guide to Stop Fear and Prevent*

Problems at the RNC, *A Promise to Help Prevent Violence at Protests and Rallies in America*, and *To and for all Law Enforcement* were written. Because of this it has Americans in need of *Ending Spiritual Warfare in America* that we are going through that divide us even more and to help us *The Recovery of the U.S. Government, The Power of Knowing "No"* that the politicians need to understand even more as days go by, plus *A Manifestation of Miracles*.

Now if the people in the rest of the world let him get under their skin too much they will need a trumpectomy from their trumphobia. I labeled trumpitis to keep them calm during the storm. It is a health message the Lord has put in place to help keep a fools from acting a fool toward the USA. The same goes for the towerist in North Korea that acts like a man baby.

Now to help cure the native ungodly American people, there has been developed ways by learning to do as the real stewards did for thousands of years before they were invaded.

A sky chief disciple can help us at home and the rest of the world with the good news about a certain problem that has been figured out and that they may not know this thing about them self or don't care?

It has its components in a way, as if the Lord is sending out his disciples to help end a kind of evolution of division. He wants us to do the same even if it is coming from our country but still letting him do what he does. It may be one of the biggest challenges we are facing in the USA. We can't fear it; we must take it on so we can see his victory.

This book is like a public relations manual. At the same time it is like a link of information that is a part of a chain reaction of love. It has different levels to become good news that is timeless to be a part of the blessings that mankind has a need of. The _All Peoples Handbook_ has been put in place to help us do this.

It has an understudy of books to help us fly the friendly skies. _A Disciple Maker_, _A Message from the Word_, _What Two can Easily Do_, _A Calling to Become Watchmen_ and _A Crown for Kings and Queens_, you can add even more books to this.

The calling is out. The world needs you. If there is a time that the Lord's soldiers need to be busy it is now. What the people of the world who are hurting because of what the people of the USA are saying need is a translation. That is why we look back to how healthy the land was and the ways the native people took care of it from following the chief. Now the land needs a new kind of chief to help stay safe from the world as much possible.

This is for all who need to know more about the Lord's will in their life regarding eternity. We can make this kind of void-noid numb-dumb sin-drome of towerism appear to disappear to stop harm. Go tell these things on all mountains from shore to shore and sea to shining sea.

To Round Things off

Be thankful to the Lord we have a platform to work from that can make things better abroad and at home.

Let's be thankful to the Lord for this grain of sand we can turn into a beach.

Fake News

If they endorse the pill Anacin at one time on "To Tell The Truth" TV show as a depression reliever then what will they say next? Did this first untruth start the revolution? If so, can we help quench the thirst of pharmaceutical companies from making their way by way of opioid epidemic and other unnecessary pain that has gotten out of control, to help stop it?

M-N

The one opening we should never go into is being docile. It is close permanently.

The goodness of progress is an unstoppable force.

Hey: don't let your time run out on you. Get it done!

Note: if they are still making land in heaven where will your land be?

Why do so many people act like they only have one life?

This piece of work can be one or all of three things depending on what level you take it. 1) The straw that broke the camel's back; 2) The straw that was used to make brick; 3) The straw that was used in the manger where baby Jesus laid after his birth.

I personally would get a straw and a milkshake and drink it all in. I don't have to be like you: can't sit still when you are going nowhere fast. It is like grasping for straws.

Now how many people have been wrong trying to defend the Lord in the past? It is not the past if some are trying to do the same today that are lost.

The ironic thing about spiritual truth is it shall be revealed even to the ones who are not willing to accept the truth. As it was when Thomas Jefferson drafted the Declaration of Independence, declaring American separation from British rule. At the same time, he was a slave owner who owned over 100 slaves.

What caused the Civil War? The belief of towerists that the church and man believe in to keep the belief that they own people to be slaves. How did it come about? The clergy and others use the Bible to fuel the separation of the nation. Now if they use the Bible to separate the country it is time we rebuild it with the Bible.

Now if you look at the history of this you will see it clearly. At the same time people don't want to accept the facts that the Lord will allow you to be positioned by your ways. Therefore, to look back and move forward if we see the past as a wrong in the land of the USA, can we stop a part of the wrong in the future? I think it is our way to a new way of life.

I will come full circle. We are again split in a way that can benefit us. If we accept the truth know there is no more North and South as it was in the past that we must move forward from. The principal of this thinking is based on one fact. The towerists that started the placement of slavery in this country are in a way still making a mark in an underlying way that must be revealed and known to all mankind in order to free a darkness that plagued our land. It has blinded the state of growth for a multitude of people from the beginning of the end of the war we fought in our land.

The past has a way of locking up some in a darkness and it creates division and separated people from themselves and the truth. This caused pain within and it has no other way out because of an undeveloped soul will spew its pain on others if no spiritual rejuvenation is taking place. As the sign of how the churches were burned and of the mosque that was under construction.

Now it showed up on little levels of hatred toward others. If we know that the loss of love comes out in hate, then we are responsible to spread it. To end as much towerism as we can and must open up the new river of love.

To make it clear, we are a nation of people whose first war was a civil war and it was really a spiritual war. Now it is uncovered that it is a spiritual war we are in now that we should not be in because the war was won by the Lord but being a lost people still in the wilderness somewhat. We are fighting against each other. That needs to be and can be stopped. Now who will know this revelation to not get locked out of the Promised Land for the current generation?

To take it a step further, the people who got trapped in an addiction are going through more than they need to, who gets caught off guard in the numb-dumb void-noid sindrome, etc.

In any given season do you give the gifts of blessing to the high places and don't go in the manger as if you were a major who came to the manger. Did the Lord know mankind was going to get lost in towerism? Of course he did but does he know who will get out of it? Renewal comes from revelation as disciples.

This is a part of the freedom from Matthew chapter 23 to point out the faults so you can get out of them.

To freshen things up, can we look at this process of growth as the catalyst that started the ending of the depression when towers fell as the song Buddy Can You Spare a Dime? That helps to bring back a new kind of spiritual growth when the country was down during the time of the depression? My thoughts you better believe it.

Stop

Now we can stop what could have been an act of suicide for the country. Start knowing a true mystery of Jesus prayer. Now who was Johosophat in your relationship?

The devil might be saying to me you plot to get my people free I can see but you know I have no authority over your Lord's work. What you say next, counts. I say I had a temporary stent only in your presence, but the Lord always owns me.

This is part of a scroll that helps to lead some to life.

9

There are too many people living in a kind of unrealistic parallel universe without truth that can come out of the sin-drome when is ripe for it to pick the truth without fear.

The Flocking Process and Super Nature
we have can Move us forward

If we think like a starling in flight we can keep out the predators better.

What may seem ironic is if we the people of the USA put a person in office then we are subject to what their losses are. Therefore, do we deserve what we get? Most importantly, do we learn from this to make things better?

One Benefit

Once you become a sky chief disciple, you are free to avoid spiritual warfare. You are also able to help lead others away from that unnecessary state of being.

A Bridge to Discipleship
(The pound of prevention we need
to help Americans with the truth)

We need to stop the next big split in the country that will come when the new tax bill gets to 2025 and the benefits are over. What will happen? The rich keep getting richer and the middle class gets cut out even more. This results in more poor people. The next president can rescind some of that if we work together to elect someone who will really represent the people.

This is the long distance blow off we get in America.

This will be the number two blow on adding to the first spiritual war we can head off and stop. We need to start now in ending the acts of a kind of spiritual apocalypse from taking place. That could become worse than the first. It can become the beginning of the downfall of the USA. Need I say more?

This is a warning from the Lord. If you think this is crazy then learn more about what can be done in the book, _To the New Wise Men_, to help put peace back together by us crossing the right bridges.

I am not talking out the side of my neck. If all I am saying is true, could this be the second wave of what could develop into a curse on America? Will it put us in line with devastation that we have no idea could come?

If the fire that has burned already, the tornadoes, the hurricanes, the climate change, etc. are leading to a kind of real depression, people may be pitted against one another which could start a kind of apocalypse.

We are not above a kind of famine or plague in our land. If we don't stop the wrong that we are doing at home and abroad.

To take it a step farther, in a way I don't want to believe that if the devil has his own disciples, then we should never let one of them run any part of the land we live in because it is a set up for a setback, even if the one doesn't know they are a devil's disciple.

Now if you understand this at all, we are being set up for the woo-woo and if we hear the Lord we can de-woo the woo-woo from knocking us down even to our needs to an unprecedented degree in life in the USA.

As a daily declaration of prayer, we all should be saying, "Lord stop me from complicating love." Then stop trying to be someone who you are not and be who you are. Then know you don't go anywhere with anyone who can't see what is right.

Brothers and Sisters, stop hanging around the opposite just to feel big.

A brief overhaul of what
Bound to Heaven Publishing/Ministries
Is offering to help make the world a better place

As author I can say that most of the 40 plus books have been written by the Lord using me as a willing vessel, even though I may have put my two cents in. The spiritual writings are some of the most timeless books that work with people to help make them and other people in the world rejuvenated on a holistic level to help the growth of humanity and continue to develop a bridge or edge using wisdom that gives foresight to succeed under all kinds of challenges. Foremost, I feel in my heart and faith that everyone who studies these guides will find what can bless them personally.

Now could it be that I have been working on a larger blessing for the people for over 40 years that amount to one of the Lord's plans to benefit mankind? Oh well, only God and time will tell what I am working with for humanity in the name of the Lord?

There are so many that can help in so many ways.
Here are a few:

To help the USA become greater we must help make the people greater first. These books and more are part of what we used to help keep the peace at and during the RNC in downtown Cleveland, Ohio in 2016. Some books were given free to the public at large. I was named as a peace ambassador.

They say the best is yet to come. One of the things, The *All Peoples Handbook* has advanced information on how to become a sky chief disciple. This may be one of the few books in the world that help to show people how to use a gift of the Lord's anointing which enhances *What Two Can Easily Do (the Holy Spirit and You)*.

Help stop the people rage problem. It is a staunch indicator that sky chief disciples are needed in America. The overall destruction and violence needs to be extinguished. Need I say more? God has opened the flood gates of peace-filled blessings that are coming in many ways. I cannot say what anyone's blessings will be but it will be worth it to invest in this way of kingdom building.

The one book to help to do that is titled *A Trojan Horse of Peace* is to help start people off in the right direction to show them where they need to be and with other books to take a ride with to end the myth, or turn it around. This book is not only turning around the myth, but helping people stop negative thinking and actions. If you describe a person or thing as a Trojan horse you mean that they are being used to hide someone's true purpose or intentions. A Trojan Horse of peace is the reversal of the traditional Trojan horse of war.

In a certain level of sky chief disciples, you can stop a part of trouble from happening with the love of God in you that you can learn you don't have to question it when you are using it.

This is for anyone who would like to give themselves a presence of a saint-like attitude in action.

My People

To help create deliverance from the fiery arrows and darts this will stop them and add discernment to your walk with Christ.

The dunamis (strength or power) spirit needs to be present more and more daily. If you don't have it you are a kind of kill joy so stop it. _The Manifestation of Miracles_ was presented through a messenger and exploded in Cleveland, Ohio gives witness to this with a clear explanation.

There are a few more books that can help in one way or another. This title reflects a positive message, _Calm during the Storm_. It is another blessed way to help ride out the storms and give people more hope in America. The next is titled _The Devil Passed Me By_ that can help show a way out of darkness to give a clear understanding of how they are produced by faith.

Favor: who is it that knows if we can show each other the Lord's favor if we are made in his image?

Get a Spiritual Health Check Up
with the Lord's Blessings

When the scandal that we have going on in America ends, where do we begin? Do we know? Yes, by starting ahead of time with these tools. To anyone who may also need the revelation of an anti-Christ prevention you can find the tools for today and the future to use as the right preventive measures of safety.

Happy days may not be here again, yet, but we can cut down on a mountain of sadness and pain by adding more and more love!

Deliver the news to help make an old world new!

A Question with an Answer

What is success and who is selfish enough to think they are a successful person and all they really are is a survivor it doesn't matter how much money you have. If you are not in the will of the Lord you are a failure in more than one way that outweigh the counterfeit labels you have placed upon yourself and you will be held accountable for it. All the money you have can't broker a deal with the Lord to fix it. Pay him now with your love or forget about the hype you have and are making today.

Check in

Now we the people can help stop leadership from spreading venom to the other people in the world. This is a place to learn how to turn around this ungodly process that weakens us on a grand scale, to let the world come to another vision of truth that frees us knowing that this plan to rebirth our credibility can be salvaged to come back from the temporary setback that Satan has put the USA under.

We can hold these truths to be evident, so we can sow the new seeds of victory as American people who can clear our conscience and put our spiritual wellness in a healthier state of growth.

The opportunity is open to not let the blessings we are afforded by the Lord and our hard work from falling by the wayside. All the world can bear witness to: all men are not created equally when it comes down to what some feel is right and it is wrong. The presence beyond the power of the positive thinking it is an omen to just do the right things.

This is not just a millennial affair. It is a re-establishment of our homeland that is undergoing growing pains. These pains can be an easier experience if we listen to all true heartfelt messages.

We have all the right tools in order to face the new process of growth to prevent a temporary setback because nothing you have will matter later; that I guarantee. Therefore, for some it is time to swallow that bitter pill that can plant a seed of a new level of life.

Stopping the consequences we are facing because of decisions we're not making. We will not fret because we can face them the right way to solve them and even head off the wrong returns that they offer.

This is not only a Christian affair,
it is a humanitarian affair!

If we can captivate a new level of spiritual peace that we can share, it is our duty to share. One of the latest writings that I have done for all who may be dissatisfied with the newly elected president and his administration. _Fixing What is Broken in America by Stopping Towerism_, another is _Ending Political Wars in America_, and the list goes on.

The latest may be one of the greatest to help all people get through the next few years and make the kind of gain in the lives of people that money can't buy. It is filled with a wealth of wisdom that was inspired by the Holy Spirit to be written and presented to show a new way to utilize the power of love. Let everyone know how much better it makes you feel. We can help the state of our country's development within the will of the Lord because it doesn't have to be a kind of four year drought when things can still be fruitful within our nation.

Anything that can draw people closer to the Lord should be embellished as priceless!

We are hoping that the leaders of the congregations help to promote these books. We are asking in the name of the Lord. It will help us continue the work we are doing and we can keep releasing the other books that are awaiting publishing. For a review of the library of books go to www.boundtoheaven.org.

Sometimes I feel as if the proud have forged rejection against me. If I have to, I will go forward alone, with the Lord.

Is this the miracle in the making people have been awaiting? This message is new for 2018. It is time to stop committing crime against one's self with this kind of prevention.

Your help is needed to stop the country from shortchanging Itself from the blessings it has to come!

Americans we are facing two levels of work: one – damage prevention, the other – damage control and recovery. We can head off some of these problems, yes we can. We must protect democracy in our young peoples' future.

Know that there is no demographics in soul relationships because we are family. This is our patriotic duty each and every one of us to look out for each other as Americans. We are the heart of our country that can help to fix it using this and other information.

The shifting change that we do foresee can give us foresight to do something about it. The work I do is only a small part that can ignite the right ways to think and go so the world will know our love for life does not stop just in America because it has always been shared with charity that will not change and cannot be changed by any man or party no matter what they do or say on any level of our government in the name of the Lord. I speak about this for him and humanity.

For those who may wonder who I am, not trying to sound sarcastic, it does not matter but who you are does matter. What can you do or are you doing to make this world a better place? If I am made in the image of the Lord then what I present does not belong to me but to us if it is of a righteous virtue. The wisdom is to help people from going foreign in their state of mind that may reflect on their actions.

These are preventive measures and steps that are prepared to help to be aware of damage that our government can or cannot do.

People listen up: we must not shortchange ourselves in the USA because we have a leader who may cause negative reactions but we can come together to keep our blessings.

So we can sow the seeds with the new life line we need to survive the storm that the whole world will not have to face. Don't be disappointed; rejoice with a peaceful spirit that gives a clear state of mind and be watchful about the truth that is within the gospel of Christ Jesus. It is yet not the end but a kind of new beginning. Is this the miracle we have been preparing for?

This can be a chapter of life to
give hope for the future!

To get satisfaction guaranteed over the next few years. It will give you a new and positive outlook.

Without brimstones we don't want to see certain things in groups of Americans so we leave them out. Now can we include them with their bows in sight with love? It only lasts 4 years then "x" out. It is time to "x" out carnage we need to sleep on the dead eye memory of yesterday.

Sometimes we have to forget the hype one way or the other in life. We will know by the deliverance of people then next thing is the draining of the swamp. It is out of sight but it needs to stop the towerists in the government of the USA. It is a time that has come by way of the Lord's mandate.

Bad tweeting is negativity that is an earthly part of spiritual warfare also to add to it the suicide that has been caused by bullying.

We

As the people are spiritually prepared. Even though I live earthly, only the Lord tells me who is president.

Real news

God has some good things going on we all need to know about them. It is time to lay the bull down to pick the people up.

Peace to the World

Do not be relating down to the judgment of self and/or others. The ball is moving forward.

This is mankind's state of hugs and pats on the back

Keep peace in your movement thank you.
The beginning again to all

As a Bird in Flight

As people of the USA should remember, the Lord may have put this burden or charge on us to help end some of the dishonest ways of the world and ourselves in order to right the wrongs of the hierarchy who think they are the mighty and have unseen lawlessness. We can know that the burdens that may have been placed on us by way of the new president cannot harm us if it is a part of the Lord's will because his burdens are light. Therefore, every time you see a bird in flight think of it as if it is the problems that are trying to be created for the country going by.

If we take the maladjustment of this process upon ourselves personally as if we are responsible the end results we will face become a burden that we create. Say "We can see the birds in flight."

Do not be a deceiver of the Lord's principles and his workings in the righteous will of mankind with the foolishness of mankind's ideals and overtures of rhetoric because of his thinking. We must not let evil come home to our presence of life. No stepping into foxholes by the country or in the country we created.

How sweet it is to hear the bells of freedom ring.

Believe one thing and see what it means
Check into the beauty without end

The Lord can put back together or reconnect the great divide of our time. This is a part of life that is coming through the space that was created for it. Act like you want to be together and you will be as one. We can reach and wake people up and away from this darkness that wants to come upon the earth today so saddle up your ride is here.

Now has so many people with towerism in America caused the Lord to treat us like he treated the people in the place called where they built the Tower of Babel and separate us because of our foolishness as he did then that left them without being able to communicate with each other and causing them to babble without being able to understand one another?

This is a stone that had to be looked under but some are picking them up and throwing them at each other even though it said he who is without sin cast the first stone and we all are sinners. That is what we can stop a big part of with wisdom.

Take a long look at least 10% or more of tax deductions that will be lost to help the Red Cross and other agencies. The *Calm during the Storm* and *How to Live with Less and Gain More* can help this also.

To keep it real we will have to step up to give to the same organizations as before even though it cannot be claimed on taxes.

Phase II

The process will help the country stop in its tracks in order to not start up any kind of spiritual warfare in the country between the people because this is what Satan wants. This is what we are denying him in Jesus' name.

How to live with less no longer and gain more

Now we haven't had much of a relationship so take what you have and do yourself proud and may the Lord bless you.

To Be Noted

One of the worse things I can say about towerists is

they are men babies, self-centered bratty people. Not all but it is a common trait and the women who have an ideology of the same toweristic views are not that way. They are more mature due to the fact of their difference in a pattern of growth. It may be like that but I am not sure due to their circular system of development by way of their natural pattern that brings about reproduction of another human.

Out

Look inside of the box and the trump even said he is a part of the problem to even add to that the airwaves of spiritual wars that he engages in with the tweeting does not help.

Women standing up

The issues of not knowing your rights is not standing up for your rights. It is using your rights not just having the blues about them to not be poor to increase your self-wealth. Women who have been put in a position of not being treated equally. The bus has been gassed up so enjoy the ride. _Calm during the Storm_ is a way to help create human rights for all to obtain equality.

The bottom line: it is a good thing to protest and rally but know the limit and if you need help please get a copy of the book titled, _A Promise to Help Prevent Violent at Protests and Rallies in America_. This book will and even more to the cause than you know now!

Give the people a chance by making this known!

To and for the people in the USA who really are in love with the country. If you are and do not fear the truth and don't want to hide it then why not learn more about who is best to run it?

This is a First Aid Kit
A Last Minute Fixer Upper

The country does not have to go through a kind of hellish situation. People must accept the truth that trump is a perfect example of someone with a sickness called towerism that the trumpees who follow him may need a trumpectomy to make them feel better.

Tip of Iceberg

Now that there is only one debate left, and the blind wants to lead the blind, can truth turn this around the right way or are we looking to punish the country because of our hatred for others or each other. The root of this problem is a spiritual element that causes a mental sickness of a kind of misguided faith that is led by their materialistic principles that people may or may not see to leave them without the right kind of moral spiritual compass.

Understanding what towerism is that functions in America without limitations that should not be. Also there is some information in the book to help you feel better with a plan that gives spiritual wellness to all people, as well as learning that accepting towerism gives a better way to understand terrorism, because lots of "isms" are dangerous.

There are people in all political parties of government

and private levels of enterprise that have towerism that need to repair this problem that we are not dealing with in our country properly.

There have been blessings received from the work I have done before! During the RNC in 2016, I promoted peace with _A Peace Offering for the Police and the _People, as well as others books to help stop confusion.

Excerpts from
"Fixing what is Broken in America by Stopping Towerism"
(With a few minor changes)

Common Sense

It is better to keep a tally on the mistakes someone has made than the mistakes someone is going to make. The bottom line is, we should forgive people and stop the prejudices.

The Negative Perspective

People can Reform the Attitude
They Have Against Self

Towerism for some can be like a drug. They get hooked on it and it has the power to pull people in that could be called a state of trumpecstasy that is a state of unseen but real kind of high that creates an invisible effect of an undetected presence of an endorphin movement in people who are powerless against it.

Keeping it real I know the country is tired and fed up

with the same old hill top bull and we deserve a change. People were somewhat surprised and wouldn't you know who comes along and beats out everyone at the table and made others look like jack legs, with a top hat that can put on a show to fool the people who think they can never be fooled. That is right, the representative of a towerist faction.

At the same time spreading a blinding kind of existence that can make some think you may need to get an exorcism before they can get themself out of the spell. Hell, I wanted to jump on the band wagon but I can't. I know the truth.

People also may think he is going to be some kind of miracle in the world for them and he may wind up with his inexperience putting the country in the belly of the whale or a battle of some kind. The USA doesn't want or need who want to know the truth.

Ohio, and the entire country don't need to have trumpitis and for those who already have it, they can get a spiritual trumpectomy.

I hold nothing personally against the Trump. He is the best example I have to help people see and know the point that is being made.

We do not need to put a person in place that can create a suicidal country.

This ship sails without water my brothers and sisters because the wins are at our backs. If you think you are the right side and you may be wrong try this.

We are not a cripple America; when we see the truth!

All of the foresight of getting ahead of the problems in life comes from the gospel of the Lord through His son, Jesus.

One of the most horrific things that happens is when a tower falls and the people within or that have put their faith in the structure of thinking get lost and get hit by the fallout of the degree of failure that tear down there faith, like the people who uses Ponzi schemes to steal but some steal the intangible willpower and trust that may be even worse. Now could it be from following the wrong leader? They have to become more scrambled as if they become more lost as was in the days when the Tower of Babel came down. It hurts and people turn all kinds of ways in their search to find themselves that left an opening in some of their souls and Satan made himself available to them and now the towerists cause some people to learn to become towerists because of the madness and sadness they feel that create more harm to people and the lands they live in or they call home.

To look even further, if our government has it warring agencies armed forces in over 150 others trying to set them on the same level as us, do we believe in this totally or do they have an underlying agenda that has towerism tied up in it in some ways? I can't say but God knows and he will deal with it one day and whoever is responsible.

Therefore the good news says let your trouble be not of a way to more destruction but let the Lord's light in to shine through to make a way out of no way in your life, because this negativity too shall pass.

This has been Developed for
Deliverance from a Dark Cloud

There so many ways to try to explain the synopsis for this new book. I hope you can connect with this; it may be somewhat lengthy; I thank you for your time.

Something about the Author

I have been in so much pain lately in my life for the last 25-30 years or longer because of the social pains it propelled me to write more to help people on a spiritual level to help myself. The pain came from not being able to help people so I write. Now can I look forward to some peace within myself? I believe so; the way I will know this is the world has more of it.

What I do helps me out of a writer's quandary that I have found myself in over one half of my life. I have worked through the quandary in order for me to escape any of my isms. I am fortunate to be free of.

The book is a guide to stop and clean up the controversy about the newly elected president. It is a way to help stop hatred of people toward one another along with the fact to show a new light that can help the government become a better place and the people be more able to get along and get things done.

This book will help people who are not happy about the way the government has been running and or the new president to grow up a lot more in the right ways plus give spiritual enlightenment to anyone who may need to add more faith and hope to their life with the blessings of the Lord.

With the power of knowing how to weather any kind of political storm over the next few years; knowing the more you know about something the less you fear.

So we are in the present when you know it is inclusion and not division that gets you in the right state of mind with others.

This therapy that the Lord has put in place for the country is of an existence and presence that can complete a state of thought. It belongs to everyone who has the will to learn of spiritual development on an old presence that has described itself in a way that looks out of the way. It is made for people to see a new kind of light in it.

The components for growth that are revealed in this book give the way out of no way that classified itself in a category that brings a peace to fix some of the broken love we as a people didn't know as much about as we needed to.

Because of our distraction from innovation we got lost out of our sight of the way a heart can escape from its pain that we need not share. This has harmed some people where their pain gives them an escape from reality that they can grow out and away from.

For me it doesn't feel good to know that it does exist. That is why this book helps so it can show a way to change to make new an escape plan from it to seek out the blind spot in one's self. It may need to be unveiled to show a way out of a hunger with a meal to put on the table of life. That is what this may do for the people.

There is a saying that you can't miss anything you never had. That is so untrue because if you miss out on different levels of love you may miss your own presence of self out of reality and it isn't a joke.

Nevertheless it does Make Sense

As adults, we should never play cat and mouse games with each other no matter whose side you are on. If we live in the USA we can learn to stand together.

We are preparing a way today for tomorrow's presence of self to weather any storm properly without the foolish acts of violence.

People shouldn't let mankind stress their endurance to a limit where it or they snap because the will in one's self has a divine order that it shares in spirit to protect it from the fact of conceding to foolishness. It is time to put your will up where it belongs in the safety of the Lord; this does help.

Without proper guidance too many children get stuck on a fairytale wishing well lifestyle. That causes them problems throughout their life that leaves them open to the void-noid sin-drone for danger to enter; this must stop. There may have been an age limits left out of this wisdom so let's know we are never too late or old to learn.

The Turning Point

To have a great society we must
teach the higher volume of wisdom

We can stop living in somewhat of a false sense of security whereby the government owns people. The people now need to learn how to own the government! I have learned that trying to change the pathway of our country takes a greater love than we have been sharing. Therefore, put your love to work for all mankind to add unquenchable hope.

The Fact is or Remains

Who cares about someone who is standing on their own convictions when they are wrong? Do not be jaded about learning from it. It is to see the truth and know it but not admit to it. It is not the more things change the more things remain the same unless you are learning from them.

The Symptoms and the Curse

This is self-prejudice caused by the lack of wisdom that people have who thinks they can misconstrue the truth. People who don't want to earn the truth in their life right now have it. The curse of the diversity of a culture does not know how to not include skin color in their practice of thinking that is one of a puzzle of pain to some but not to all.

To Begin 2018

The bottom and top line to it is that we don't have to put ourselves into a perpendicular reality that has appeared and should not phase us as Americans and only God knows the level of our personal presence in the governing of our lives.

This may be a part of the people who are caught

between the cataclysms in their mind to pray for. This is the beginning of a new kind of quantum leap that may land you in a heavenly state of mind if you are one of those people.

This may be one of the best ways at this time in history for people to lay claim to their spiritual equity that they were born with, without going through some kind of hellish situation to bless the Lord.

Actions to Believe in

Knowing we all can be led to do the will of God. How strong is your faith? Can it become able to carry the score of the Holy Spirit?

Some of the books that have been completed for over the last few years have given notice about what is taking place in the country and world. They offer some simple answers to why along with some solutions.

The Lord says for us to be holy because he is holy. Follow the Lord!

1 Peter 1:16
16. because it is written, "Be Holy for I am Holy."

Hear Ye, Hear Ye

In this new year of 2018, it is to be known the blessings of the Lord by way of his personal gift he has to bestow upon you individually to learn what yours may be.

Is this the true test that we have as Americans have

been waiting for? Is it our time to learn how to be the real judge and jury that passed sentence upon the people and land we live in? Has it come down to the people leading and not the elected officials because we pick the right leaders?

Now what can you do to help fix one of the upcoming problems the US is facing to help sew up the fault line that is spoiling the very ground we are walking on as if it is like a hole that one day will open up and God only knows how many will fall in and get hurt.

I will go over this again. The first opened up with the Civil War only had a makeup process done to it. The latest one opened up more in ways that some can't see since the new president was put into office but it is number two. He will be gone out of office and the three 3 will open up and that is where we all in the USA come in to sow the seeds of victory by not letting the country get split more apart from the bad air and the land cost increase from taxes.

The earthly process of the people not having a fault line so no one is pointing their finger at someone else because no one wants to accept the blame for the mass that is going on. That way a fault lie or line does not appear and we help it disappear that wants to separate the USA even more.

Next, by using this wisdom we don't get into the spiritual war with the prince of darkness so that the Lord can step up and defeat it as he has planned for Satan.

Now how nice it is to not be blinded by foolishness and to avoid the traps Satan has set up for humanity within a reasonable amount of time. No that is not right; time is of the essence on the wisdom now starting today. The more who know the more are saved.

To become a watchman for the Lord with prayers is now needed. What is first? Pray for the president of our country to have sense enough to do the right thing along with the leader of North Korea to do the right thing because talking about playing with fire lots of people could get hurt. Lately, the USA has had enough fire to put out because of people not wanting to have anything to do with us. Some people hate our guts and the current president is not helping to stop this.

We can stop the anti-American dislike that is taking place around the world.

This may be looked at like evolutionary genetics on a spiritual basis of logic in action to prevent destruction.

Let it be known that I am not creating condemnation against anyone. I am helping to teach people to not do unto others as they might do unto you.

Harmony

Get in harmony by stopping the things that continue to divide us that makes us toxic toward each other and this is what this information can help us to do.

The loss that we have in our country is not talked about but it slaps us in the face day in and day out. It is the pride we once had that has been given up by the ugliness that we have let speak for us. Now it is the time we let the Lord speak for us through us.

This book reminds me of a book I wrote over 15 years ago, _A Kaleidoscope of Knowledge_. It had a theme to inspire the youth to pull their pants up. Why would I say that? It is because this book does the same in its own way to let the people in America know keep their pants and pride up and stay on their p's and q's in order to stop Satan from sneaking up on us to do us harm in more than one way.

To read the book that was written for teens will open your mind even more. Now the last thing is this may seem like a jig saw puzzle that can help you put the pieces together, believe it or not.

To fulfill the big picture get the full meal of spiritual food to soar above the clouds and fall up into them that help create the real trickle up affect.

This information should be treated as a serious matter as it is a plague in the land. At the same time, it is ending due to the fact that we have just won a spiritual war before the fight began. Look at it as we did when the Germans surrendered at the same time our resistance to the plague started to end in the people in the country dying and they stopped but even the people in the parade in the year 1817 in California wore face masks to add protection.

Now we are to think like we have been given a halo to protect use with wings because there is no more plague and no more war.

This Book is Non Fiction

I have written on this subject before and I will write about it again because it seems so appropriate.

I was a child and with my father and one of my brothers walked in the back woods of Alabama and Mississippi and we came upon a great lady. She was called a soothsayer. She told my father to take care of me because I was going to do great things. I heard that and I felt as I grew up she touched me then and now in a way that I was passed a set of tools; a staph or a scepter and needle and thread to sew that can't be seen. One more thing to be used as a gift as she has shared with me that I am now sharing with you and you one day past the same to others.

It is my hope that the wishes you have for to receive the right way to go can now be seen even more daily as my sight has manifested.

This may be one of the least organized books I have produced but to be truthful, I believe it is complete, regardless of the way it presents itself. The reason for this is I am tired and after 44 plus years of writing I needed a break since I have at least 5 to 7 more that have to be put to bed.

Do we know if we can reach higher ground?

This is a gift from the Lord to America, written by the Holy Spirit, co-authored by Bro. Bush. It will help create foresight that helps the growth of future generations.

Avoiding the Pitfalls that may Lead to Hell

To think like the Lord is what Satan is trying to do. It

will never be because it is not real. He thinks he is the king of the warlords in the universe. The king is peaceful and full of love not hatred. Again, he thinks he has a kind of trinity under him and that is made up of death. Who can they be? One thing only. People who are lost out of God's saving grace, even though they have not been committed to Satan's kingdom as long as they are alive on earth with breath in their bodies.

Toweristic views

It can harm the way people think even if they are not a towerists. The shame of it all is when people don't want you to help them.

Here are Satan's biggest adversaries/patrons that can do the most harm as they live in a kind of wilderness.

The three t's: 1) the terrors; 2) the towerists; 3) the toweristic people. They have a level of others who fall under them and between them that will be mentioned next.

The worse part of this is people are warring with themselves no matter how much love they have or are giving out in the world. When you go or grow against the Lord's will it is that way, like it or not because you can look good but be a false representative of true reality. Who else is in the family of the t's I mentioned? 1) towers falling; 2) terrorists; 3) treasonous people, and there are more.

Everything that is going on in the White House I have written about in other books. I hope you have the opportunity to read them. This presentation of information will help people stop terrorizing people and let go and let God do his thing in the heart of mankind.

This book is like a rook that moves into your life with its knight in shining armor to stop the crook by putting Satan into checkmate.

To help inform our government we should email them about all the things that can be learned from this ecumenical ministry of knowledge to help them stop the madness that creates sadness.

It is time to stop feeding into the "he say" "she say" gossip in the White House b.s. and stop wasting time on the numb-dumb crap that others have going on in their life.

It is time to replenish the nature of mankind with a new kind of freedom and armor that the Lord can provide.

The right attitude gives the heart an extra measure of pleasure of no guilt that is like an outreach center of emotional growth that is contagious to all people. Enjoy life and live to let others understand your enjoyment also.

Now, let us not make the same old ungodly choices. We can help our own civilization make it to the next millennium because we have done and are doing our inner homework for our spiritual growth. Thinking you know and knowing you know are two different things. So maybe acting like you know is the best thing to do.

Get Off this Pathway

We can re-address some of the inequity in life that are not fair to the moral standard of living. It is always conditional love that has their causes in mind. It is in their family also not just the people around them but they won't admit it and/or use a loved one and let them go. There is no unconditional love anywhere if it comes from towerism: it is the nature of the beast.

No real control of self, equals abuse of power and abuse of authority and people. People act like they don't know and don't want to know that Satan controls a part of them.

The misuse of power – dumbing down and bullying people. It is time to grow up your intellect. There are at least seven billion people on earth. In America, we may have been placed in a position to be responsible for helping to develop an ecumenical spiritual plan of growth that can affect the majority of them.

Some people may call this a process of mindfulness because it minds the mind to get the jewels out of it but it can still do much more; meditate on this.

Note: once your extra sensory perception becomes clearer, you will be able to see and read between the lines to know the stage of growth and the working of a process of growth as it takes place.

This process of wellness can help the entire country reach a new place of peace to show the world our re-united spirit.

What the Heck
(Trump/Bannon)

It is really shameful to have a couple of so-called grownups act like two foolish and devilish kids: one minute they are best buddies, the next enemies for life.

Not to be Over-looked

As American people, we now have to be subject to watching two towers fighting and worse doing it in front of the world. If this doesn't make us look bad nothing can. Therefore, who is lying about whom or who is telling the truth? It really doesn't matter because the presence of both of them has created enough chaos to last a lifetime. We need to be ignoring it because both are towerists.

Where is the Help that is needed for our President?

Are we ready to face the truth about what is in our hearts or not? They say or the Lord said to love your enemy. Therefore, if you understand that someone is their own enemy and they don't love themselves, what can be done? One thing is to teach them to love self. Our president has a problem and doesn't seem to know it. Do we harm him for it or act like he is our neighbor? If we know better we help. We have to help them to understand their wrong. Pray for them and try to explain what makes sense about what they are doing that is not good.

Looking at the whole situation of what is going on in the Trump man's life. He is under attack and may be heading for a fall. He is a towerist and if that be the cause he is not a person who will go down without a fight. Therefore, what fight will he go all out on, with the people in Washington, the media, the other nations, North Korea?

The one he must not choose is the one who causes him to push the button. We are his best levels of understanding to keep him on the right path to stop the devil from pushing him overboard. The analogy of this can be made simple. No one needs to drown in their own mess.

If we can see more than one truth can we see two wrongs at the same time? We know one person who helped the president get elected to office was with the help of Steve Bannon. Now did he help him knowing that he was who he was and would do what he does just to set him up for the woo-woo? Did he capitalize on the numb-dumb void-noid sin-drome state the president would be in knowing they didn't get along? One day he would have the dirt on him to spit, piss, shit back in his face because of jealousy and the fact he couldn't be in the house to get his snake on anymore.

If all that is true, then the fight was created before they were ever in the White House. The spy in the game was never anything but a high ranking way to come back to capitalize on the fact of them creating the mountain they try to make out of a molehill in a way to gain wealth one way or another. I have said before there is a book to help stop a crook but for the first time I will say it is a book to help feed a crook? I have said it before, I have sat in on Satan's camp as a spy to help get a way out for the people. In another dimension this is what Bannon did and doesn't that take the cake? This will take the Trojan horse and put it on the right level.

The British are Coming

Before the horse rode in with Paul Revere

The emancipation had been put in place; the beginning of the end of a relationship that had come to a head. The Brits that were towerists had other towerists in America. One side wanted to tax the other, but there is no honor among most towerists because there can only be one person at the top of the tower. We fought against the Brits to keep the power we assumed we earned to be a free land with others.

We look at the power in the twin towers, Trump and Bannon fighting for power. They became what they were meant to be in the first place, traders. They used each other as much as they could to gain whatever they could from each other.

Now comes the fact of how the devil was in the details all along. It is time to spew venom. Who is the snake and who needs the Lord to step in to be their shrink and help them think right? Do you know or is it both of them?

I was just thinking that the last president was a man of no drama. Now we have one full of nothing but drama. I said we must work with what we have like it or not.

What is one of my biggest issues? It is to help Trump get out of the tower he is in and lessen his chances of hitting his head on something and accidentally hitting the button. Even though it is okay for him to fall on his butt.

The next thing is for the people in the country to get back on track and stop being so nose-driven because of the lacksidasical state of watching the two towers because we lost the twin towers in New York because of being in that state with all of the toy shopping and joy popping we did. Wake up America. This is not the time to act like an airhead without a plan.

It is Not okay to Sit back

What we have going on is to help all people so they don't fall out of the towers they are in. This past year has so many different kind of people falling: Lauer, Smiley, Weinstein, Rose, etc. before them there was Cosby.

This is only one group of people on one level. There are so many levels out there. The ones who can help themselves need to. Some who are on other levels may need more help to see their problem so they can identify with it.

Last but not least, how many people are afraid of the towers they serve under? If there is one that is too many. If there is one who is a coward it is time for courage. There is no excuse for being a wimp.

We must protect America
(even from those within)

It is understandable to be afraid of losing a job and income. But to give up your manhood and wimp out over something that affects peoples' lives, it is a shame if you let another person dictate your morals. It is wrong and you are wasting your life away. How many phonies and towers are there in the White House that are blinded to what is going on?

We pray to make sure the president doesn't crack his bulb.

Read this book two times maybe backward the second time.

This is a no-nonsense book. No one gave their permission to use their name.

Time is up for towerism all over the world.

To put it as plain as I can, I was the main person who took down a man named Hightower at an early age. In my neighborhood he was a rapist/murderer. Now I am helping them down in another way that doesn't take violence.

People who brag on their own smartness have a problem of some kind.

This may be a holy relic written before our time

They say it is time to become learned about how to take your place as a sky chief disciple in order to be able to fulfill the skyways to release the cupids throughout the world to stop the stupid from harming others. Also to be able to stitch up the rip in the valley where the green grass can grow even more to know the still waters that run deep and clear that bring peace to the soul of humanity.

To show the Lord that you are not afraid of your personal anointing and gift may be one of the wisest things to do in life. If you want to know more about this ask the Lord and he will tell you.

Now and then you can shout hallelujah that you are making room for the comforter to come into your life more and more daily. Now put some of this icing on your cake in life.

When all is Read and Done!

Your faith will cleanse you so you can enter a new atmosphere within to be able to walk in righteousness in the spiritual wisdom of the Lord.

This new book helps to redefine re-correlate recalculate the American spirit. It helps it to see into new ways to add light to what may be a pathway that holds a kind of darkness that is misplaced that needs to be seen before people walk onto it, whether it is a day from now or years from now or how it came about.

One of our number one goals is to get to as many people as we can that have towerism and get them to get a towerectomy. This sickness that is of a spiritual origin can be cured. It will make the world a better place. It will stop lots of mankind's destruction. Keeping in mind one thing, people need to change the fact of giving up their free will for the Lord's will in their life.

The fact of the matter is when people got stopped from building the Tower of Babel, they got mad and sad because they don't understand why they can't reach an unobtainable goal in a pretext of not wanting to have limitations like getting to heaven. They think they are some kind of super supreme human in a subconscious dream state. The DNA of this spiritual problem went forth to curse mankind and it has not visible   to the naked eye but not to the spirit that exists in mankind and has done more damage than it should have done. Now the Lord says stop it.

One of the biggest benefits of this that we have learned is it can bless mankind. Also, it is people approved and as a kind of illness the prescription does not have to be FDA approved because it is already approved by the Lord.

It is time to make known the problem that exists in our society because of creation of sexism by men, who are in 90% (or more) cases can be label, towerists. In combination to what is going on we can set two caged birds free at the same time that kills the beast of burden that has plagued mankind for too long already. Now one is no worse than the other; when you check it out.

When people sit in high places who may think down inside that they are in an upper room which is made for the sanctified people and not the satanized people who don't mind living with wrong in their life or they don't realize that they have been paralyzed from the right way to grow.

I figured it out: people who speak too highly of themselves are too smart or dumb for most peoples' good.

Now the easing down of the towers who are acting
like they are falling is what we need to be doing to
help them along with the fact that there may be a
couple of towers bumping into each other at the same
time. That can create a fallout that can harm others.
As an example, Trump and Kim Jong Un.

Book Note

What is one of the reasons also that may be
happening when the president is so high off an
ungodly atmosphere that he live in it has him swaying
in his state of balance. It comes out in his speaking
out of the side of his neck. Remember, he is trying to
do something he had no business doing in the first
place. His ego pushed him up into a place he did not
need to be.

There is _Calm During the Storm_ that written over a
year ago to help put out the firestorms that the
president puts a blaze to. Thank God he has a
backup plan already in place to put the firestorms out.

This book is not complete without your input that adds
happiness to the world and to help the planet's
ecosystem improve. Therefore, bring your gift to add
to this one.

This is a renewal plan for people, the country and the
world showing that the Lord still forgives us so we can
make things better.

Your help is needed to stop the country from
shortchanging itself from the blessings it has to come!
The top and bottom of this is the Lord has blessed
America now it is time for America to bless the Lord,

and the house of God's people need to be first to do this.

The time has come to put a stop to one of Satan's strongholds that he has on mankind. It is a place of a kind of unawareness that takes and captures them. It is the unfamiliar state of towerism. It is a blinding force that needs to be reckoned with on a Godly level.

We Don't Have to Let Go of our Blessings if we have the Right Plan

There is a chain reaction of things going on in the country that are linked to one another. They not only make us as Americans look like fools but causes us to act like fools. The agenda on this has been hyped by the president, Trump, and other people in different ways. This is not easy to deal with and now we have to break the link in the chain of events by dividing the problems to work through them.

I have concluded the process will take a number of levels of therapy that can be received through the latest books I have authored.

The Old Hindsight Made New

This may sound like some kind of MacGyver principle, but it is a spiritual law of relativity. The more you know about the darkness inside of a dimension of what was lost, the less power it has over you and others. Now it is like the mummy that was buried in a tomb for thousands of years. You don't know about it until it is opened to you. This was a kind of tomb that the Lord had raided to let the light of truth in and stop the harm that it had once done.

This work of knowledge is like a person that wrapped their arms around you if you let them. It is timeless with song like a singer who won the 2017 awards, being Tony Bennett.

The truth about the way I write is, it is not on a conventional level. It has a process of delivering a message as if it is a text book that recommends other books and as if it is a classroom setup. Therefore, please take notes to review after reading the complete book.

Isaiah 43:2-3
2. When you pass through the waters, I will be with you; and through the rivers, they shall not overflow you. When you walk through the fire, you shall not be burned, nor shall the flame scorch you.
3. For I am the Lord your God, the Holy One of Israel, your Savior;

Acts 20:24
24. But none of these things move me; nor do I count my life dear to myself, so that I may finish my race with joy, and the ministry which I received from the Lord Jesus, to testify to the gospel of the grace of God.

Philippians 4:17
17. Not that I seek the gift, but I seek the fruit that abounds to your account.

Notes

____

____